INSPIRATIONAL ADULT COLORING BOOK

Cattitudes

PURE PURRRFECTION

MAJESTIC EXPRESSIONS
Relax, Refresh, Renew

BroadStreet
PUBLISHING

INTRODUCTION

Research shows coloring is an effective stress reducer.
Maybe you picked up this book because you've heard the
hype and you're curious… like a cat. Perhaps you've been
looking for a way to relax. Now you have your very own
adult coloring book, and you have every reason you need
to sit down and color.

Cattitudes. There are plenty of them. Those we would
be wise to imitate are purrrfectly illustrated in this book
featuring our fantastic feline friends.

Coloring is a great distraction from all you have going on,
but the best way to find lasting peace is to spend time
with your Creator. As you fill these intricately designed
illustrations with the beauty of color, dwell on the richness
of his Word, the faithfulness of his character, and the depth
of his love for you.

RELAX. REFRESH. RENEW.

LOYALTY

"Because he loves me," says the Lord,
"I will rescue him; I will protect him,
for he acknowledges my name."
Psalm 91:14 NIV

PATIENCE

Imitate those
who through faith
and patience
inherit what has
been promised.
Hebrews 6:12 NIV

CONFIDENCE

I can do everything through Christ, who gives me strength.
Philippians 4:13 NLT

ASSURANCE

We can confidently say,
"The Lord is my helper;
I will not fear; what can man do to me?"

Hebrews 13:6 ESV

UNDERSTANDING

Blessed are those who find wisdom, those who gain understanding. Proverbs 3:13 NIV

Examine everything carefully;
hold fast to that which is good;
abstain from every form of evil.

1 Thessalonians 5:21-22 NASB

CURIOSITY

FAITHFULNESS

Let us hold tightly without wavering
to the hope we affirm,
for God can be trusted
to keep his promise.
Hebrews 10:23 NLT

SELF-CONTROL

1 Corinthians 10:13 NLT

God is faithful.
He will not allow the temptation
to be more than you can stand. When you are tempted, he will show you a way out so that you can endure.

NURTURING

Satisfy us in the morning with your unfailing love, that we may sing for joy and be glad all our days.
Psalm 90:14 NIV

ENTHUSIASM

It is always good
to be enthusiastic
about good.
Galatians 4:18 HCSB

DETERMINATION

Be on guard. Stand firm in the faith. Be courageous. Be strong. And do everything with love. 1 Corinthians 16:13-14 NLT

JOYFULNESS

The Lord has done
great things for us,
and we are filled with joy.
Psalm 126:3 NIV

GENTLENESS

Let your gentleness
be evident to all.
The Lord is near.
Philippians 4:5 NIV

CONSIDERATION

Be kind and loving to
each other, and forgive
each other just as
God forgave you in Christ.
Ephesians 4:32 NCV

WISDOM

If any of you lacks wisdom,
you should ask God,
who gives generously
to all without finding fault,
and it will be given to you.
James 1:5 NIV

Trust in the Lord and do good;
dwell in the land and
cultivate faithfulness.
Psalm 37:3 ESV

GOODNESS

COMFORT

May your
unfailing love
be my comfort,
according to
your promise
to your servant.
Psalm 119:76 NIV

GENEROSITY

Let each one give as he purposes in his heart,
not grudgingly or of necessity;
for God loves a cheerful giver.

2 Corinthians 9:7 NKJV

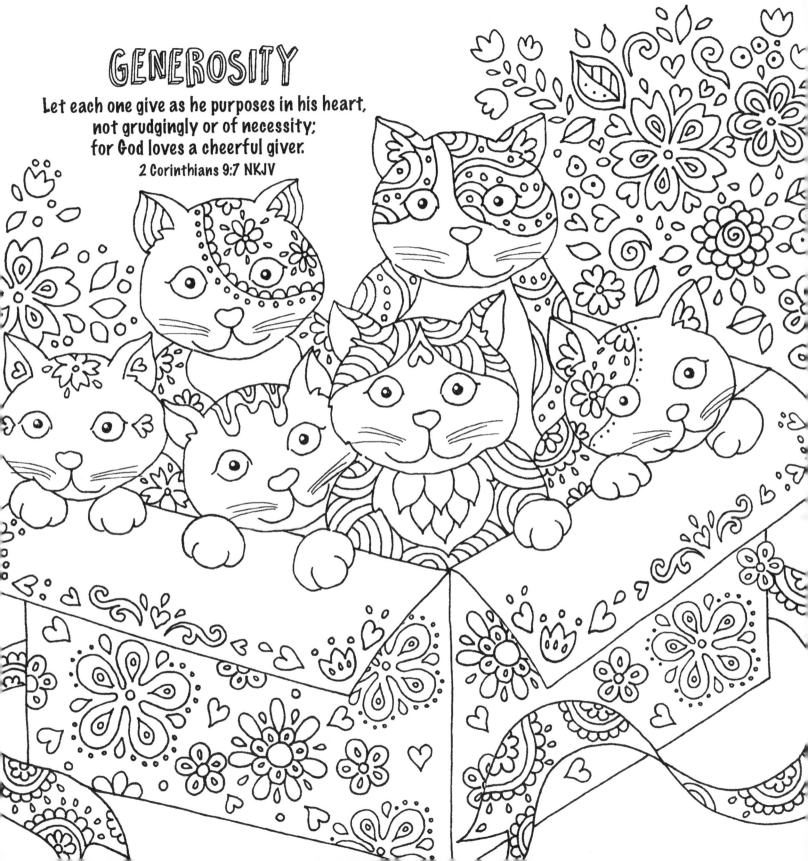

In peace I will lie down and sleep, for you alone, Lord, make me dwell in safety.   Psalm 4:8 NIV

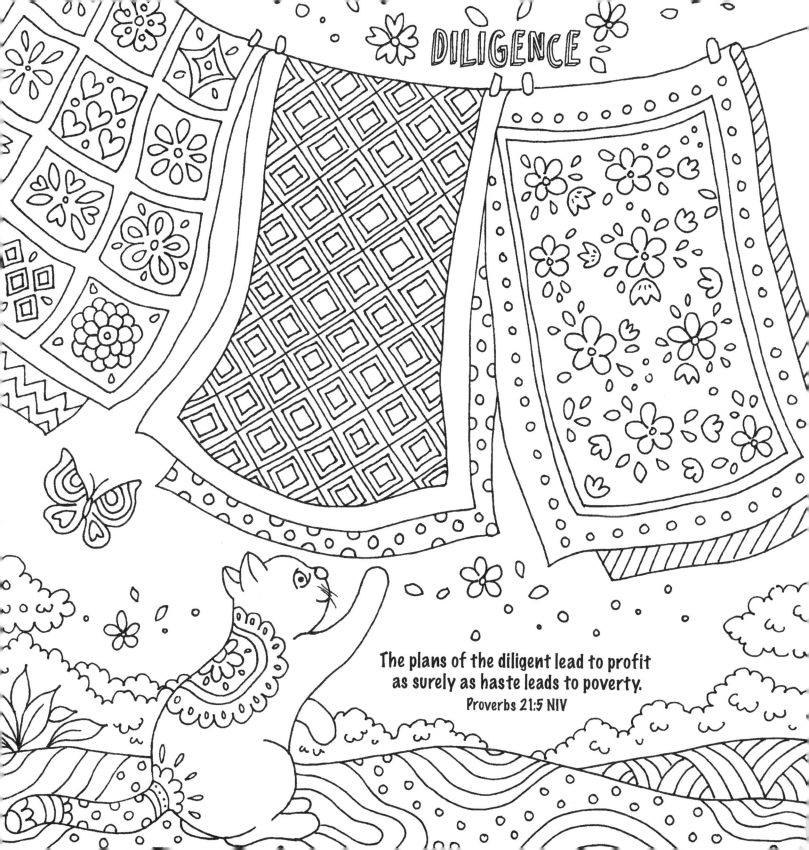

DILIGENCE

The plans of the diligent lead to profit
as surely as haste leads to poverty.
Proverbs 21:5 NIV

STRENGTH

Be strong in the Lord
and in his mighty power.
Ephesians 6:10 NIV

THANKFULNESS

I will give thanks to the Lord
with my whole heart;
I will recount all
of your wonderful deeds.
Psalm 9:1 ESV

COMMITMENT

May your heart be fully
committed to the Lord our God,
to live by his decrees and
obey his commands.
1 Kings 8:61 NIV

CONTENTEDNESS

"Seek the Kingdom of God above all else, and live righteously, and he will give you everything you need."
Matthew 6:33 NLT

UNITY

How good
and pleasant it is
when God's people live
together in unity!
Psalm 133:1 NIV

BENEVOLENCE

The generous will themselves be blessed,
for they share their food with the poor.
Proverbs 22:9 NIV

ORDERLINESS

Each of you should continue to live in whatever situation the Lord has placed you, and remain as you were when God first called you.

1 Corinthians 7:17 NLT

SERVICE

Use your
freedom
to serve one
another in love.
Galatians 5:13 NLT

Make my joy complete:
be of the same mind, having
the same love, being in full
accord and of one mind.
Philippians 2:2 NRSV

COOPERATION

COURAGE

Be strong and courageous.
Do not be frightened,
and do not be dismayed,
for the Lord your God
is with you wherever you go.
Joshua 1:9 ESV

PERSEVERENCE

Let us not grow weary of doing good, for in due season we will reap, if we do not give up.

Galatians 6:9 ESV

TRUST

Trust in the Lord with all your heart,
and lean not on your own understanding;
in all your ways acknowledge Him, and
He shall direct your paths. Proverbs 3:5-6 NKJV

HELPFULNESS

Galatians 6:2 NIV
Carry each other's burdens,
and in this way you will fulfill the law of Christ.

FUN

You will show me
the way of life,
granting me the
joy of your presence
and the pleasures of living
with you forever.
Psalm 16:11 NLT

CREATIVITY

Having then gifts
differing according to
the grace that is given
to us, let us use them.
Romans 12:6 NKJV

LOVE

1 Corinthians 13:13 NLT

Three things will last forever
-faith, hope, and love-
and the greatest
of these is love.

EXCELLENCE

In all the work
you are doing,
work the best you can.
Work as if you were
doing it for the Lord,
not for people.
Colossians 3:23 NCV

PLAYFULNESS

She laughs
without fear of the future.
Proverbs 31:25 NLT

INTEGRITY

The godly walk
with integrity;
blessed are their children
who follow them.
Proverbs 20:7 NLT

COMPASSION

As a father has compassion on his children,
so the Lord has compassion on those who fear him. Psalm 103:13 NIV

Truthful words stand the test of time,
but lies are soon exposed.
Proverbs 12:19 NLT

HONESTY

Don't look out only for your own interests, but take an interest in others, too.
Philippians 2:4 NLT

TENDERNESS

PURITY

All who have this eager expectation
will keep themselves pure,
just as he is pure.
1 John 3:3 NLT

FORGIVENESS

"If you forgive other people when they sin against you, your heavenly Father will also forgive you."
Matthew 6:14 NIV

PURPOSEFULNESS

Proverbs
16:4 ESV

The Lord has made
everything for its purpose.

CLEANLINESS

Create in me a clean heart, O God,
and renew a right spirit within me.
Psalm 51:10 ESV

COURTESY

Be of the same mind toward one another.
Do not set your mind on high things,
but associate with the humble.
Do not be wise in your own opinion.
Romans 12:16 NKJV

FRIENDLINESS

Let us consider how to stir one another to love and good works,
not neglecting to meet together, as is the habit of some,
but encouraging one another.
Hebrews 10:24-25 ESV

TRUTHFULNESS

Let us not love with words or speech,
but with actions and in truth.
1 John 3:18 NIV

HUMILITY

Humble yourselves
in the sight
of the Lord,
and He will
lift you up.
James 4:10 NKJV

RESPONSIBILITY

Pay careful attention to your own work,
for then you will get the satisfaction of a job well done....
We are each responsible for our own conduct.
Galatians 6:4-5 NLT

Ascribe to the Lord the glory due his name;
worship the Lord in the splendor of his holiness.
Psalm 29:2 NIV

RESPECT

RELIABILITY

Commit everything you do to the Lord.
Trust him, and he will help you.

Psalm 37:5
NLT

MATURITY

Do not think like children.
In evil things be like babies,
but in your thinking
you should be like adults.
1 Corinthians 14:20 NCV

BroadStreet Publishing Group LLC
Racine, Wisconsin, USA
Broadstreetpublishing.com

MAJESTIC EXPRESSIONS

Cattitudes

© 2016 by BroadStreet Publishing

ISBN 978-1-4245-5305-1

& interior design by Chris Garborg | garborgdesign.com
piled and edited by Michelle Winger | literallyprecise.com
ration design by JP Winger and Jared Winger

nted in the United States of America.

17 18 19 20 21 22   7 6 5 4 3 2 1